The Ultimate Guide to Top Quality College Planning

INSIDER SECRETS
that save you Time and Money…
FINALLY REVEALED!

Katherine O'Brien, MA CCPS

The Ultimate Guide to Top Quality College Planning
Copyright © 2012 by Katherine O'Brien, MA CCPS

Disclaimer

The purpose of this book is to educate. Neither the author nor the publisher guarantees that anyone following the techniques, suggestions, tips, ideas, or strategies contained herein will be successful. The author and publisher shall have neither liability nor responsibility to anyone with respect to any loss or damage caused, or allegedly caused, directly or indirectly by the information contained or not contained in this book, or in any of the companion products.

ISBN-13: 978-1482060294
ISBN-10: 1482060299

Printed in USA.

Dedication

I dedicate this book to my beloved children: Sean, Fiona, Margaret, Liam, Colin, and Brendan. Thank you for all of your love, support, and sacrifices! You are the greatest blessings in my life – and my best teachers!

You are the reasons I am an entrepreneur and am committed to helping bring out the best in every person I work with. You are why I refuse to give up on my dreams. I want to be an example to you of being true to your authentic self. I love you with all my heart!

Acknowledgements

My heartfelt thanks to James Malinchak, who helped me recognize the importance of writing this book in order to share my knowledge with more parents.

I am also grateful for the guidance I have received from my friend, coach and mentor, Rae Majors-Wildman and the input I received from my friend, Robert Parkerson.

I am also most grateful to Mark Berdan, without whom this book would never have even been started.

To my friends who have stuck with me through thick and thin over the years. Valerie and Rose, you have helped me stay the course and I thank you.

I am grateful to Mother Teresa, MC, who is my mentor in so many ways. Your example of starting with nothing but love and a sense of God's purpose yet making a tremendous difference in our world is one I am doing my best to follow. This book is an important early step in that process.

This book would not have been possible without the love and support of Jesus Christ, my Lord.

Table of Contents

About Katherine O'Brien, MA CCPS

Katherine O'Brien, MA CCPS, known as America's Leading Authority on College Planning is the founder and principal of Celtic College Consultants. With nearly a decade of experience, she has served hundreds of families all over the USA, saving them countless hours and thousands and thousands of dollars. Katherine coaches teens and their parents to identify their dreams, then their dream schools. She guides teens to discovering themselves then manifesting that greatness. She guides them as they unveil it on their college applications. Her clients have received hundreds of thousands of dollars in scholarship aid

She has worked with families from every educational background: homeschool, charter school, military, public schools, and private schools. She meets with her clients via the Internet, over the phone, or face to face.

With over 13 years' experience as an educator, Katherine brings a wealth of experience to her clients. She is making a positive difference in the lives of college bound families all across the United States. Clients love her focus on bringing out the best in their child as well as her incredible ability to find schools with merit money for them.

She is an award winning speaker, empowering people to live powerful and fulfilling lives manifesting their passions, gifts, and talents. She is an inspiration to many. Katherine also speaks about leaving the shackles of living in fear and confusion. Her passion is helping people discover their purpose in life, and empowering them to live bold, fulfilled lives in accord with their purpose and passion. Her talks have been warmly received.

Katherine has given countless workshops and webinars on various college planning talks for years. She has spoken to many audiences in person and online. She earned two standing ovations at James Malinchak's College Speaker Boot Camp in 2012 and was honored by Barbara Niven for her speaking achievements.

Katherine is the mother of six children ranging from 18 to 8 years of age. They live in Southern California.

Katherine holds an MA in Theology and Christian Ministry from Franciscan University of Steubenville as well as a BS degree in Industrial Engineering and Management Sciences from Northwestern University. This multifaceted education enables her to work with students across the spectrum of academic fields with great effectiveness.

 Each section of the book starts with a boxed summary and ends with an action item.

Introduction

Parenting a teenager is a daunting task. Having four myself, I thoroughly understand! The high school years are so much more complex and stressful than they were just a few years ago and a world apart from when we parents were teens. The stresses come, fast and furious, to our children at far younger ages than ever before. And our kids aren't any more ready for these challenges than we ourselves were.

Working with a college consultant can relieve some of the difficulty and tension, as well as make a soother path, since they've guided many families on their journeys to college. College consultants, generally, are trained professionals who bring additional skills and knowledge to the situation. When you work with a college consultant, you find yourself no longer needing to rely on the talk amongst the parents you know and some hopeful guesses. Families find themselves enjoying the high school years, rather than panicking their way through them, paying late fees and hoping it will all somehow work out. All too often they find themselves buried in debt only a few years later! Thankfully, there is a wide array of professionals available to help. These professionals have various specialties and varying degrees and areas of training and expertise.

Since college consultants work with students and their families, it is imperative that parents have some idea what to expect, as well as what to watch out for. Unfortunately, some college consultants are prone to be unethical, just as professionals in every other arena.

The Ultimate Guide to Getting Top Quality College Planning was written after meeting with numerous recipients of detrimental college planning advice (both financial and college selection and admissions). These families were more desperate than ever. Recovery was often impossible, given the short amounts of time left before their children were to start college and the actions which had already been taken.

Hopefully, you'll find the help you need in this guide so your journey to college is a smooth and satisfactory one.

This book is a guide, and only a guide. There is no substitute for your own wisdom, research, and common sense. I make no guarantee that every possible pitfall has been pointed out. I have, however, done my best to provide an effective guide for your child(ren)'s journey to college.

After most chapters you will find a page to record your notes. I am always writing in books so thought these would be helpful to you. There's a lot of material here and there are bound to be questions. If you'd like to discuss it, see the "Our Gift to You" chapter.

Finally, I'd like to share an old Irish blessing with you:

May the road rise to meet you,
May the wind be always at your back.
May the sun shine warm upon your face,
The rains fall soft upon your fields.
And until we meet again,
May God hold you in the palm of his hand.

May God be with you and bless you:
May you see your children's children.
May you be poor in misfortune,
Rich in blessings.
May you know nothing but happiness
From this day forward.

May the road rise up to meet you
May the wind be always at your back
May the warm rays of sun fall upon your home
And may the hand of a friend always be near.

May green be the grass you walk on,
May blue be the skies above you,
May pure be the joys that surround you,
May true be the hearts that love you.

We're lost! Who can help us??

When meeting with prospective college prep professionals, it is important for families to ask about the scope of their services, since they vary so widely from one planner to another.

College Planning professionals are called:

College Planners
College Admissions Consultants
Higher Education Consultants
Independent Education Consultants
Certified Educational Consultants
Certified College Planning Specialists
College Consultants
College Processing Consultants
College Counselors
College Funding Consultants
Education Consultants

These are some of the many titles used by professionals who assist students and parents with college and financial aid planning. Some of these professionals work for high schools, some for colleges, and some are "independent." Independent college consultants and planners work directly for families just like yours.

In general, admissions consultants only provide student preparation services including course selection, college selection, and application review. College funding consultants, on the other hand, often never meet the student. They only provide investment advice. Some admissions consultants also offer some level of financial aid advice.

College planners are skilled in helping students find colleges where they can be successful. They also serve as guides to the college application process, making sure that students meet deadlines and prepare complete and effective applications. Some higher education consultants specialize in helping students with special needs, such as learning disabilities or NCAA/NAIA scholarships, or finding merit aid for students.

Some college planning specialists assist families with college funding planning and financial aid eligibility as well as the financial aid application process. A few college planners or college planning firms work both with students and with the finances.

College admissions consultants tend to specialize in student preparations for college and college selection as well as the admissions process. They often provide no guidance to families regarding funding strategies and the financial aid process.

In college planning firms, it is common to find that different people handling different parts of the process. That specialization can have some benefits, however, their clients lose the benefits of having a college planning specialist who understands your family's entire scenario.

For example, an affluent family with a high EFC (Expected Family Contribution, calculated based on the financial aid application) will have little or no financial aid eligiblity. However, they may have lots of highly valued assets but may also have very limited cash flow. Having a planner recommend that their child apply only to very expensive schools with no opportunity for merit aid, may well mean that the child won't be able to attend a four year college, because there simply won't be adequate funding.

Another family, with high need, will need to approach the college selection process differently. If there is not a strong connection between the financial and student preparation professionals in a big firm, these nuances will be lost, costing the family aid and, perhaps, making it impossible for a student to head off to college with his or her classmates.

 It is best, therefore, to work with a planner who is holistic, providing both student preparation and college funding services.

Notes

Should we do this on our own?

> *In order to get the best results, every athlete knows that he or she needs a coach. So it is for college bound teens.*

After all, you may be thinking, with the Internet, we have access to incredible amounts of information. We can look at the admissions requirements as well as other people.

All of that is certainly true. However, getting accepted into college is far more difficult than it was when we parents were in high school. Back then we picked a few schools, put together our applications, and got acceptance letters galore. However, even for "average" colleges, the competition is fierce.

On the other hand, in the US, there is a college for every student. Unfortunately, many of them have extremely poor graduation rates. Even the President has addressed this and put incentives into place to reward colleges for graduating students and penalties for those which seem to have many students who end up with debt but no degrees

In short, in order to get the best education for your particular student at the lowest possible cost to your family, a college planner, a trained professional who focuses his or her life on this area will be an invaluable partner.

Lastly, at this time, in the US there is an enormous population of students who drop out of college. After a semester or two or three, they are disillusioned, lost, confused, and depressed. A few, sadly, commit suicide. On the other hand, students who have a defined purpose and goal for their life do much better, both at staying in college and at finishing their bachelor's degree in four years. Don't you think you'd like your child to be one of those kids, rather than one of the first group?

 It is best, therefore, to find a college planner you are comfortable with who can direct you and your teen along your journey to college.

Notes

Watch Out for Scholarship Scams

> *Never pay for scholarship searches. Be sure to search for the right kind of scholarship money.*

Some college planners offer parents a scholarship search service. Unless you have a personal valet, don't bother. You and your student can search for his or her own private scholarships on the Internet and in the library. There is absolutely no need to employ a professional college planner for this task. If you really don't have the time, you could probably hire a conscientious person you know to do this for you at a much lower rate than a professional planner.

It is critical that you make distinctions between the types of scholarships available. There are private scholarships – these are monies offered by private individuals and organizations. They typically require that the student complete a project and report on it or that the student write an essay. Private scholarships must be reported to the colleges and, usually, will lower your student's financial aid award, dollar for dollar, because they increase your EFC (Expected Family Contribution.)

Private scholarships are considered Resources by the financial aid formulas. Resources are added to the family's EFC, because they increase the family's ability to pay.

Your student's time is precious so should be directed to the most effective means of lowering college costs and increasing available funds possible.

Additionally, every college and university creates its own policies. At many, outside (private) scholarship monies are offset within the financial aid award by a reduction in institutional scholarships (from the college or university itself). Families, naturally, would prefer that any loans in the financial aid package be reduced first. Unfortunately, the schools do not usually handle it that way. Consequently, your hard won private scholarship may well not reduce your actual college costs at all.

Seventeen percent (17%) of all financial aid money comes directly from the colleges. These come in the forms of tuition reductions, grants, and scholarships directly from the schools. Some of these awards are based on financial need; others are based on other criteria and are called "merit aid." Be aware that some merit aid has a need component so is not strictly merit aid.

 Hire a college planner who understands the impact of private scholarships on financial aid eligibility. Hire a planner who can guide your efforts, knowing whether it will benefit your family to actively seek private or institutional scholarships.

Notes

"Free College" – True or Scam?

> *Anyone with good credit can get 100% college funding. In the real world, we call these loans!*

There are some financial planners who work with families preparing for college who advertise that they can get families **100% funding**. That is true for all US citizens (and registered aliens) with good credit; the PLUS (Parent Loan for Undergraduate Student) loan program allows parents to borrow any needed funds up to the cost of attendance. (The COA or Cost of Attendance is the total cost for one year of college: tuition, fees, room, board, books, supplies, travel, and incidentals.) Years ago, a colleague of mine worked with a family who'd recently filed for bankruptcy, after putting two children through college on their VISA. So, 100% funding is out there by various means but is not a prudent college funding plan, to say the least.

Just the other day, I saw an online ad from a major credit card company (one of the top four) offering student loans to cover up to 100% of college costs – at fixed rates as low as 6.7%. Unfortunately, it is all too easy to bury yourself in debt. This can be disastrous to your future, especially your retirement years.

The PLUS (Parent Loan for Undergraduate Studies) loan program is run by the federal government. Through this program, parents can take a loan each year for the entire cost of attendance, which includes tuition, room, board, fees, and books, less any grants or scholarships. Clearly a loan is NOT "free" schooling! From a cash flow perspective, it is "free." At the current 7.9% interest rate, a loan is not free!

A year at college at an "average" cost school costs approximately $30,000. If your student only takes four years to graduate, that's $120,000 in loans, at 7.9%. Over 10 years, you will repay a total of $173,951.65. In order to make those payments, a family will need to earn $175,000 per year, in order to only use 10% of its gross income to repay the loans!

However, on average, it takes students SIX years to complete a bachelor's degree. That makes the loan amount $180,000. Paying back $260,927.47 over ten years doesn't sound like free, does it?

Before we move on, please note that the average amount of indebtedness of college graduates has been significantly increasing each year. These young people are starting off their adult lives in bondage to their student loans. Some are unable to find employment which pays enough to live on and repay their loans. Many of these students are returning home. They can't marry their sweethearts (if they have one) and launch into their adult lives because of the tremendous burdens they have. With proper college planning, these situations can be avoided and student and parent debt minimized. It is absolutely essential to look at the long term scenario of both parents and child(ren).

 Hire a consultant who provides guidance truly in line with your family's long term best interests. Find one who

provides net cost predictions based on the average past performances (percentage of need met, percentage met with gift aid) of the colleges.

Notes

Oh No! Hidden License Shell Games

> *Parents MUST ask about the credentials and licenses of every person in a prospective planner's company.*

Many college planners who help with financial aid and/or college funding planning are not simply college planners. Having expertise in various financial and insurance products which can be used to fund college can be beneficial. However, there is an inherent conflict of interest faced by those professionals.

Sadly, over the past couple of years, I have worked with families who were given advice that seriously undermined their ability to pay for their child(ren)'s college expenses. These wolves in sheep's clothing advisors directed their clients to move funds in ways which did not benefit them for college, but did yield the planner/broker/agent a nice commission. In some cases, they have reportedly recommended products which make the family's college funds unavailable during the college years. I was absolutely shocked when I saw this!

If the planner will not tell you whether s/he or the firm has a license, take the time to look up his or her name and the firm's name on your state's department of insurance website. If they have a license and don't let you know up front, you need to seriously question whether they are worthy of your trust. After all, they are legally required to put their license number on their business cards and websites. If they deceive you at this point, will they give you sound advice?

If you do choose to work with a college planner who is a life insurance agent or financial planner, it is imperative that you get a second opinion either from your existing agent or a referral from a friend or trusted colleague (or your CPA, etc.) on everything he or she recommends! Commissions can be very high on life insurance and fixed or indexed annuities. Additionally, it is important that you consult with your CPA prior to making any changes since there may (or may not) be tax consequences. It is very important to explore cash flow, tax, and financial aid consequences of any proposed action.

You may not realize it but your financial aid eligibility and your AGI from your taxes are fundamentally linked. Both the PROFILE and FAFSA formulas use your AGI (from the full calendar year just prior to the school year in question), along with other information, to calculate your EFC (Expected Family Contribution.) You are eligible for financial aid to cover the costs of a given school which exceed your EFC.

 If you desire financial aid and funding planning, hire a planner who does not sell financial or insurance products but who has good relationships with individuals and firms who do. ALWAYS get a second opinion on investment advice AND consult your tax advisor before doing anything.

Here's a true story of a family I consulted with during the 2011/2012 school year (slightly altered for privacy reasons):

There was a family who went to a free college prep workshop held at their son's high school. The workshop was given by a non-profit organization. The family subsequently started to

24

work with XYZ College Planning***. Because the workshop was at the school, the parents assumed the school had vetted the group. In fact, that is almost never the case (and it wasn't in this case, either). Additionally, most people think that non-profit organizations are "safe." The truth is that many for profit businesses use non-profits just to get into the schools. Having a non-profit doesn't mean a company is ethical (or unethical) or that their products or services are beneficial to you.

In the beginning, their son had meetings with "Sally" from XYZ. He and "Sally" worked on SAT and ACT prep, course selection, and college selection. They met regularly and got along very well. "Sally" was a very nice lady and seemed quite helpful. The son trusted "Sally" and his parents became very comfortable with XYZ College Planning.

After their son had been working with "Sally" for about six months, "Tom" from XYZ College Planning contacted them and they started to also work on financial planning for college. The first thing "Tom" did was advise them to refinance their home and take $100,000 in equity and move it into annuities, since annuities are not assessed for financial aid. Mr. and Mrs. CollegeBound did that. It cost them some closing costs and some effort but they thought it would be worth it so they did it happily. They would do anything to help their son go to college. And they were desperate for help.

The next time they met with him, "Tom" advised them to change their life insurance plan. When they contacted their life insurance agent about it, she consulted with me about the situation and then extensively researched it. When she met with Mr. and Mrs. CollegeBound, they learned a great deal.

The first thing they learned was that the equity in their home would not be assessed for financial aid on the FAFSA form so moving it into another non-assessed vehicle did not benefit the family at all. Their son was not planning to apply to any schools using the PROFILE form so the fact that home equity is assessed by that formula did not affect them at all. In fact, the home equity, which could have been accessed to pay for college was now tied up in an annuity with high surrender charges (big fees to get the money out) and penalties (if the money was removed before either parent was 59 ½.) Being younger parents, they would have incurred both the charges and the penalties to access the funds formerly available through a line of credit on their house.

Secondly, their agent also informed them that, although this investment shift did not improve their financial aid eligibility, "Tom" at XYZ College Planning was due to make $35,000 in commissions on this transaction.

Thirdly, their life agent explored XYZ's website and other materials and did not find a single instance where it was stated that "Tom" had life insurance license (which also allows a person to sell annuities.) By law, that information MUST be disclosed. So the CollegeBound family, like many, had been hoodwinked. They had no idea that their college planner was giving bad advice and making enormous commissions "on the back end." Because of their early interaction with "Sally", they had come to trust XYZ College Planning implicitly.

There's one more lesson in this story for you. The XYZ College Planning firm has a non-profit branch. That non-profit entity has the ability to have workshops in the schools and to distribute marketing fliers through the schools. That was how Mr. and Mrs.

CollegeBound heard about the workshop that was held in the school library. And it was the fact that it was a non-profit organization that solidified their credibility with Mr. and Mrs. CollegeBound. Unfortunately, they found a wolf in sheep's clothing, not the top quality professional assistance they needed and paid for.

***XYZ College Planning is a completely fictitious entity.

 MORAL OF THE STORY: Don't wait to get advice until you are desperate AND be careful to evaluate all of the implications of any recommended actions, particularly if your college planner will be making a commission on the transaction.

Notes

Too Good to be True?: Guarantees

> *Only the Financial Aid Office can guarantee a certain amount of aid.*

Anyone can **guarantee of $5500 in aid**. $5,500 is the maximum amount for a Stafford freshman student loan*, an entitlement of every US Citizen and green card holder. All you need to do is file the FAFSA (Free Application for Federal Student Aid) form for each year of college and your student can take these loans, no matter your income or assets.

A good college planner is well versed on the financial aid rules and procedures. S/he can guide you to maximize your need based financial aid eligibility.

In fact, fully 17% of all financial aid monies come directly from the colleges and universities in the form of tuition reductions, scholarships, and grants. Working with a planner who is adept at matching students with institutional scholarships as well as maximizing your aid eligibility will benefit your family tremendously.

Finding schools which are a good fit for the student, have a net cost within your target, and a good chance at non-need based merit aid takes concentrated effort. However, we have found, year after year, that the rewards are certainly worth the effort.

If your student is an athlete who is seeking a college scholarship, there are special rules to follow, starting with registration with the NCAA or NAIA. According to the NCAA, only 2% of high school athletes go on to pay college sports with a scholarship. Consequently, having financial back up plans is <u>essential</u>!

* for the 2013/2014 school year
** Students need a credit score of 0 or at least 620 to obtain private student loans.

 Hire a planner who will maximize your need based as well as your merit based financial aid.

Notes

How do we pick Schools?

> *"Tunnel vision" will cost you! Pinning your hopes on one school is a bad plan.*

Each student and family is different. Consequently, it is imperative that the college selection process be tailored to each student. Different factors will come into play for each search. Unfortunately, many planners have certain "go to" schools that they encourage all of their clients to include on their list. That sort of "cookie cutter" approach does not serve your child very well.

It may be the case that you and/or your child have particular schools in mind. A good planner will help you and your child determine if those are good fits for him or her. Even if they are, creating a robust list of competitive schools is essential. Remember, you want the schools to need to compete with one another in order to win the prize – your student. (and your money!) That competition often takes the form of institutional grants and scholarships.

With it now taking an average of six years for American students to earn a bachelor's degree, helping students find schools which are good fits for them is essential. It doesn't benefit anyone to have young people wandering around college campuses aimlessly for an extra two years.

Many people, even after getting a degree, don't really know what they want to do. Some of these young people move back in with their parents, others take jobs which they don't like. This lack of enthusiasm at work often manifests in poor performance and fewer advancements as well as lower satisfaction with life in general. Some of those people will return to school later in life to prepare themselves for a career change. Others will simply live dissatisfied lives.

A good college consultant is willing to invest time and effort with your child in helping him or her recognize his or her gifts and talents and discover a profession (or range of professions) to which s/he is inclined. Then her or she will take the time to find the proper academic setting for your student.

 Hire a college consultant who sees your child and family as unique and is diligent in finding the proper college fit.

Notes

We need Less Stress!

Bringing a college consultant into your life should bring a great relief from stress!

The high school experience is overflowing with stress and pressures unheard of when we parents attended high school. A college planning specialist will strive to reduce that anxiety for both students and parents. A good planner will not belittle a student's academic and extracurricular accomplishments. S/he should strive to be sensitive to your family's dynamics. You and your child should be comfortable when interacting with the consultant, whether in person, online, via text or phone.

Professional consultants strive to work as a team with families, high school counselors, and college admissions and financial aid offices. They respectfully and skillfully guide students through the application process, offering feedback on applications and essays, but never writing the essays for the student.

Working with teens is a privilege. Those with a different attitude are not good choices as your college consultant. Putting the best interests of teens at the fore can be challenging. They don't always have the best attitude and can be difficult to work with. A planner who loves teens will have patience and wisdom to bring to each situation.

Hire a planner who views working with teens as a privilege. Find one with whom you and your student are comfortable. This is just as important as finding an ethical, competent consultant!

Notes

How do we tell who is who?

> *The consultant should demonstrate college admissions and financial aid related knowledge, experience, and training.*

Most college consultants have acquired some formal training. Some have not. Most also belong to one or more professional organizations. In this section, you will find descriptions of the professional organizations. Following it will come descriptions of the various formal training programs currently available.

Do NOT skip this section. It's critically important that you understand the background and skills of any college planners you consider working with. There is an incredible array of programs and organizations, each with different strengths.

An "independent education consultant" is one who works for families, not for a specific school (high school, college, or university.) These consultants are hired directly by families like yours to assist them with the college prep process.

Good college consultants participate in professional organizations such as the Higher Education Consultants Association (HECA), the Independent Education Consultants Association (IECA), the National Association for College

Admissions Counseling (NACAC) and/or one of NACAC's regional affiliates, the National College Advocacy Group (NCAG), the National Institute of Certified College Planners (NICCP), and/or the National Association of College Funding Advisors (NACFA).

In order to help you understand the scope of the various professional organizations, below are brief descriptions of each, along with their websites.

HECA (Higher Education Consultants Association) is a national organization of independent college planning professionals. Independent college planners do not work for high schools or colleges, but directly for families. Members must be college graduates with paid college consulting experience.
(http://www.hecaonline.org)

IECA (Independent Education Consultants Association) is also limited to independent college consultants (those who work for families, not schools). IECA has several tiers of membership and requires extensive campus visits for full, professional membership. Professional IECA planners have been on at least fifty campuses in a three year period. IECA professional members must have a master's degree and typically spend about 20% of their time visiting various college campuses.
(http://www.iecaonline.org)

NACAC (National Association for College Admissions Counseling) and regional ACAC groups are open to college admissions staff, independent consultants, high school counselors, as well as professionals in related fields (e.g.,

test prep companies). NACAC and its regional groups put on excellent college fairs around the country, as well as professional development conferences. A planner who belongs to NACAC and/or a regional ACAC is demonstrating some level of exposure to college admissions and financial aid staff.
http://www.nacacnet.org

NACFA (National Association of College Funding Advisors) is focused on the college funding side of college preparation. From the president's online biography, we learn that NACFA is '"one of the fastest growing insurance marketing organizations in the entire country." **If you choose to use a NACFA affiliate, be aware that you are working with an insurance salesperson.** NACFA provides training to its advisors, who must also attend monthly teleconferences. NCAG is currently developing a certification program for independent college consultants.
http://www.mynacfa.com

NCAG (National College Advocacy Group) is a group of independent college consultants working together to assist people in making informed decisions in all areas related to higher education. NCAG offers high quality monthly educational webinars. NCAG members tend to be very well informed due to the strong emphasis on continuing education. (http://www.ncagonline.org)

NICCP (National Institute of Certified College Planners) is focused on the financial preparations needed for college but does include admissions as well. Members of NICCP have earned the CCPS designation. In general, one must be a Certified Financial Planner (CFP) or Certified Public Accountant (CPA) in order to be eligible to become a CCPS.

Their focus is helping financial professionals add college planning to their business to generate leads and new business. Seasoned college consultants are also permitted, on a case by case basis, to earn the CCPS designation. Certified College Planning Specialists are required to complete 24 hours of continuing education credits each year. (http://www.niccp.com)

Credentialing programs:

CEC - Certified Independent Educational Consultant
University of California at Irvine's Extension Program offers this certification program for independent education consultants. It has an admissions focus and includes some need based financial aid training, but no funding strategies. The program can be completed completely online.
https://unex.uci.edu/certificates/education/iec/

CEP – Certified Education Planner
The American Institute of Certified Educational Planners offers this program. In order to attend, you must have a master's degree, recommendations (to ensure high ethical standards), and pass an exam. The program has an admissions focus and is designed for school employees, not independent planners.
http://www.aicep.org/
http://education-portal.com/certified_educational_planner.html

CCC – Certified College Counselor

UCLA's Extension Program offers an online certificate in college counseling. This program is primarily intended for school counselors. It is admissions focused; however the financial aid fundamentals are taught. CCCs must hold a bachelor's degree.
https://www.uclaextension.edu/collegecounseling/Pages/default.aspx

CCPS – Certified College Planning Specialist

NICCP (National Institute of Certified College Planners) is primarily focused on the financial preparations needed for college but does include admissions as well. Members of NICCP have earned the CCPS designation. In general, one must be a Certified Financial Planner (CFP) or Certified Public Accountant (CPA) in order to be eligible to become a CCPS. Their focus is helping financial professionals add college planning to their businesses to generate leads and new business. Seasoned college consultants are permitted, on a case by case basis, to earn the CCPS designation. (http://www.niccp.com)

Additionally, no matter his or her credentials, ask prospective college consultants you are interviewing for references and/or former clients you can contact, as well as professionals whom the planner partners with or recommends. Take some time to explore his or her LinkedIn connections and recommendations and Facebook pages (personal and business). Check for Yelp reviews, too. Just as in anything else, you can learn a great deal about a person by the company he or she keeps.

In addition to credentials, the college consultant should provide testimonials from previous clients whom you may contact for more information. It is very important that you take the time to explore these references and testimonials. Speaking with families who have worked with the planner you are considering will give you valuable insight into his or her methods, in addition to a sense of the type of results real people just like you have had when working with the planner.

Notes

What will you do for us?

> *College preparation is a collaboration between the consultant, the parent(s), and the student. Have clarity regarding who will do what and when it will be done.*

In order to obtain effective results, clear definitions of expectations and responsibilities, as well as open communication are essential.

College consultants provide an incredible variety of services. Some only assist with applications and essays. Some also provide college selection guidance. Some provide financial guidance but don't work with students. Many who work on the admissions side don't touch the financial aid or funding sides; some will do financial aid but have no idea what funding strategies might benefit their clients. Some work on an hourly basis; many offer package plans of varying types.

Given the spectrum of services provided by college consultants, it is imperative that parents have written agreements or letters of engagement. The contract must define the services to be provided, a timeline (when they will start and end), which student(s) are being served, as well as the payment arrangements.

There is nothing worse than missing a deadline because of a breakdown in communication or mistaken expectations.

Consequently it is imperative to have clearly defined responsibilities.

A very good practice is to have the student sign the agreement, in addition to the parent(s). By their signature, the student is affirming his or her willingness to cooperate with both of his or her parents and the consultant. After all, without the student's participation, the process will fail. Additionally, this action sets the tone. Preparing for and attending college are both major steps toward functioning as an adult in society. Making and keeping commitments is a fundamental skill needed to be a successful adult and this small act is one small step on that journey.

It is reasonable for a contract to include termination details. On occasion the relationship does not prove to be effective. Students, from time to time, refuse to cooperate. Plans and situations may change as well which may make college planning services unnecessary.

Consequently, it is absolutely imperative that you learn exactly which services a given consultant will perform for you, and what he or she will not be doing for you. Clearly defining modes and times of communications is also essential to forming a successful professional relationship. Having the fee schedule clearly explained is also important, naturally.

Additionally, the engagement letter or contract must include some language regarding the protection of your personal information. Your planner should be very comfortable with all of this. The best college consultants bring these issues to your attention, making clear how they protect your confidential information.

Hire a consultant who clearly defines the scope and duration of services, as well as the fee structure and termination details, in writing.

Notes

Check those References!

Insist on the highest ethical standards!

Since college consultants deal with highly personal and sensitive information, it is imperative that your planner be a person of integrity. Verify whether he or she has a broker's license by checking his or her name at FINRA.org. Check his or her firm with your local Better Business Bureau. And, absolutely explore his or her LinkedIn account and Facebook page(s). Professional references are also very important. Take the time to check them.

Remember, the consultant will have social security numbers, often have tax returns, account statements, and the like. It is essential that you take the time to verify their trustworthiness. You'll also need to confirm with him or her how she handles files once your student has gone off for college. How long and securely are they stored and how are they disposed of?

Some consultants belong to the National Ethics Association. (www.ethics.net) While such a membership can be a good indication that you are dealing with an ethical person or business, checking references, etc. is still mandatory. Anyone, can join the NEA for a modest fee. Consequently, membership is no guarantee of good character.

Additionally, the engagement letter or contract must include some language regarding the protection of your personal information. Your planner should be very comfortable with all of this. The best college consultants bring these issues to your attention, making clear how they protect your confidential information. Be sure to confirm protection of electronic, paper, and any other versions of your information.

 Hire a consultant of the highest integrity and one who will protect your sensitive information.

Notes

Can we talk?

> *Your college planner must be able to communicate with you AND your teen effectively. That includes listening carefully to you, as well as expressing themselves.*

You need to be able to understand what your consultant tells you, be able to clarify things, and ask all of your questions.

You need to be heard. If you direct the planner to look for colleges with a certain geographic, religious, athletic, or other factor, you need confidence that you'll be given what you have requested.

A coach is not helping if s/he does not give an accurate assessment of the strengths and weaknesses of the person s/he is coaching. If you go to a golf pro, it will not help if he tells you that your swing is great and you just need to spend more time on the driving range. When you continue to slice your shots, or shoot erratically, you know there are defects in your swing that need to be addressed. Only by providing an honest and accurate evaluation of your stance and swing can he help you.

So it is with the college consultant. It may be painful news to hear that your child has little to no chance of acceptance at his or her dream school but, the truth is better than applying to the dream school and similar schools and ending up having no acceptance letters. As painful as the news is when it comes during the college selection phase, it offers the student the opportunity to improve his or her test scores and the overall admissions profile before applying, rather than just being rejected by a beloved first choice school. The student can also focus on schools which are more likely to accept him or her, thus achieving the overall objective of collegiate study in the student's desired field or major.

Remember, the best thing a college consultant can do for his or her client is to give honest assessments and candid feedback (nicely delivered, of course!). The coachable client will then work to improve his or her admissions credentials as well as shift the schools on his or her list.

A good coach will have several ideas regarding how to improve the deficiency in meaningful ways.

The same sort of honesty is also essential on the financial side of things. If your consultant isn't able to give you beneficial, concrete help lowering your EFC, if possible, qualifying for merit aid, what your net costs are likely to be, whether a given financial aid award has grounds for negotiation, he or she is not being effective.

 Hire a consultant who will be honest with you and your student, no matter the news.

Notes

Are you Coachable?

> *Working with a consultant requires an ability to collaborate and be coached on the parts of the parent(s) and the student.*

Something for you to consider before engaging a college consultant is whether you and your student are willing to take direction from others. In order to collaborate with a college planner, you must be able to follow directions and listen to, evaluate, and act on the professional advice you are given.

Some indications that you and your child are coachable are these: Do you use a tax preparer? An investment advisor? A golf coach? An aerobics instructor? A business coach? Have you taken an adult education class recently? Has your teen worked with a sport coach, theatre director, etc. well during high school? Do they listen to their Scoutmaster or youth pastor, etc.? These sorts of activities show an ability to be coached. If you consistently figure things out on your own, refuse help, or consider yourself a rugged individualist, you may have difficulty working with a college consultant. If you have difficulty receiving constructive criticism, working with an educational consultant will be difficult. If your teen is overly stubborn or terribly insecure, collaboration may be difficult.

In general, high school students tend to be fairly responsive to adult direction. Sometimes parents lose sight of that fact, since their teen is pulling away and trying to do things on his or her own. However, they are generally coachable by other adults, even if they tell our kids the very same things we told them.

Take a few minutes to consider how well you and your teen are suited to working with a college planner.

 In order to successfully work with a consultant, the parents and the student(s) need to be willing to take direction from him or her.

Notes

Can you Match My Learning Style?

> *Matching learning styles is key to successful collaboration.*

In recent years, many people have become more familiar with the various learning styles. Some people learn better by doing. Others learn more effectively when pictures or images are used. A wall of words, or a long lecture is ineffective for both of these types of learners.

Conversely, some people remember what they hear. These people can recite movie scripts after only watching it once. They can replay conversations in their head. Lastly, some people learn best by reading. Imagining scenes they are reading about does not come easily to them.

Synesthetic people are multi-dimensional. For them, colors have texture, scent, etc. Their awareness is blended and on a different level from most people's.

Because there are so many different styles of learning and communication, it is important to work with a planner who quickly identifies these, and can shift his or her modality effortlessly. This is critically important. It is common for one family to present two or three different styles. In order to effectively work with both parents and the student, the consultant must be able to address each effectively.

This ability is very obvious when it is time to select schools. Some are focused on the feel or look, while others on facts, while others on the people they met. Pulling these different perspectives together and helping the family decide which schools are the best fit overall, which are most in accord with the family's defined goals and priorities is essential to successful college consulting.

In addition to the various learning styles, personalities must be taken into consideration. If a consultant is too demanding or direct, or unclear and unmotivating, he or she may not be right for you.

 Hire a college consultant who is adept at working with people with differing learning styles and who has a repertoire of motivational techniques.

Notes

Conclusion, Directories, and a Note on Fees

As you can see there are many, many different things to keep in mind when you are researching and interviewing potential college consultants.

You are now equipped to hire a college consultant well suited to your needs. You know what questions to ask, what to look for, and what to expect. You are now able to find a college consultant who can provide the outcomes your situation requires.

Additionally, keep in mind your teen's true needs. Some teens are comfortable working on their own, with minimal guidance while others require weekly in -person conferences to keep them focused and making progress. Keeping these sorts of things in mind will help you when you are considering working with a planner like myself, who works with families throughout the country, or realizing you need to find one in your local community.

Several organizations provide directories of college consultants. The NICCP's guide to CCPSes is found at: http://parents.niccp.com/search.asp. NACFA and regional ACACs do not have member directories and NACAC does not have a directory accessible by the public. Happily, NCAG offers a free, accessible directory here: http://www.ncagonline.org/Main/advisors.aspx.

HECA's directory is available online at this address: http://hecaonline.org/Directory. IECA only lists their

professional members in their directory located online at this website:
http://www.iecaonline.com/cfm_PublicSearch/pg_PublicSearch.cfm?mode=entry.

Working with a college planner can be a sound investment of time and money and provide an excellent ROI (both monetary and in terms of improved quality of life (less stress!). Student outcomes greatly improve and, if your planner is skilled at it, your savings should more than compensate for the consultant's fees.

As with everything else in this field, you will find a wide range of fees, from $14,000 for a one week application prep camp to $75/hour. Choosing a college consultant solely by price is a mistake, unless your rule of thumb is to hire the most expensive one you can afford. As with most things, you get what you pay for.

Notes

Useful Websites

College Prep Tools by Katherine O'Brien, MA CCPS
    Campus Visit Guide
    SAT/ACT Essay Guide
    Student Resume Guide and Examples
    College Selection Guide
    Discounted Online Test Prep Courses
    Admissions Prediction Program accounts
Www.celtic.infusionsoft.com/

Organizations with Directories of College Consultants:

National College Advocacy Group
www.ncagonline.org/Main/advisors.aspx

Independent Education Consultants Association
(Directory does not list associate members)
www.iecaonline.com/cfm_PublicSearch/ps_PulbicSearch.cfm?mode=entry

Higher Education Consultants Association

www.hecaonline.org/directory

Other Useful Websites:

FAFSA EFC estimator:
www.FAFSA4Caster.ed.gov

For articles on a variety of college prep topics:

www.collegeprepanswers.blogspot.com
www.unigo.com

For parent and student dialogues on college topics:

www.CollegeConfidential.com
www.unigo.com

SAT
www.CollegeBoard.com

ACT
www.ACTstudent.org

Having Katherine Speak to Your Group

If you, your employer, school, homeschool group, or organization is ready to step up to the next level of service to the parents in your group, you have no alternative than to invite the premier college planning speaker in the US, Katherine O'Brien, to speak at your next conference or event. To discuss scheduling and arrangements, please call her San Diego office at (858) 705-0043. Ms. O'Brien speaks on a variety of college prep topics as well as teen and young adult empowerment topics.

Our Gift to You

Your free One Hour Initial Consultation ($300 value)

This is our gift to you to help you gain clarity. We will discuss your (student and parents) personal situation and goals and how we can help you achieve those goals.

What is your commitment to your future? Remember that knowledge is only potential power... it becomes real power when you take Action!

Visit www.CelticCollegeConsultants.com and click on the contact us tab to schedule your free initial consultation. Be sure to let us know that you have read this book; it will make our conversation much more effective.